GREEK COOKING

JG
PRESS

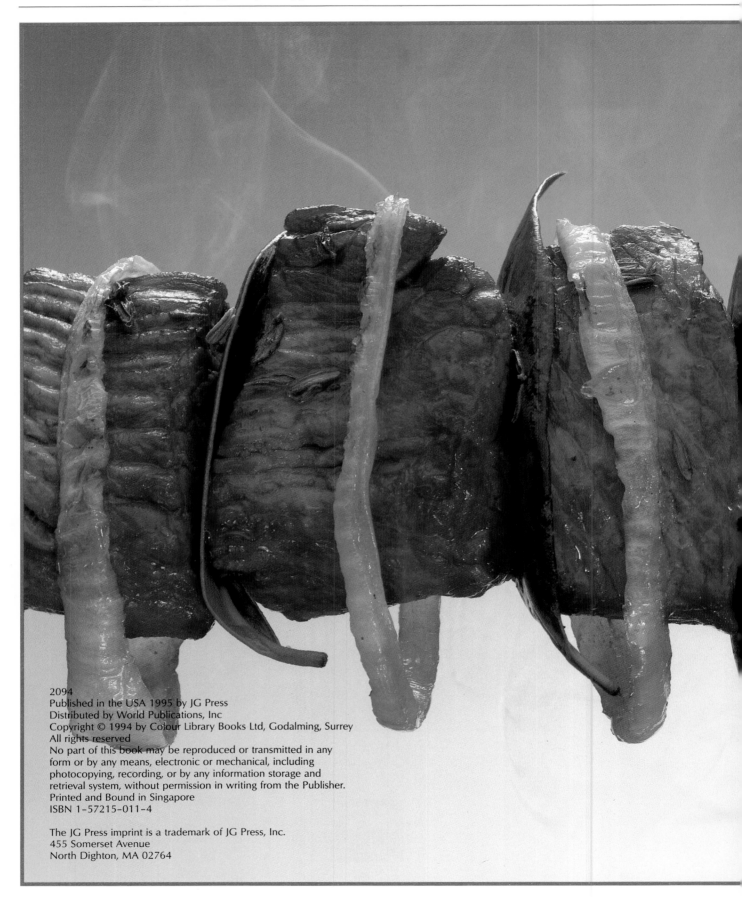

2094
Published in the USA 1995 by JG Press
Distributed by World Publications, Inc
Copyright © 1994 by Colour Library Books Ltd, Godalming, Surrey
Printed and Bound in Singapore
ISBN 1-57215-011-4

The JG Press imprint is a trademark of JG Press, Inc.
455 Somerset Avenue
North Dighton, MA 02764

INTRODUCTION

Greek cookery has much in common with that of other countries which share the Mediterranean climate, and yet, it is different.

Herbs are used liberally — oregano and basil being the favorites — but the resulting taste is not Italian. Spices, such as cinnamon and coriander, figure prominently, but the taste is not Middle Eastern. Olives and olive oil are essential ingredients, but the taste is not Provençal. The taste is undeniably Greek, and reflects all the vitality of the country and the belief that food is part of life and to be enjoyed without pretensions.

Greek recipes rely on the freshest possible ingredients prepared to let the natural flavors shine through. Eggplant, zucchini and artichokes all speak of the warmth of the country, and are used in many delicious ways. Olive oil is an essential ingredient and lends its fragrant bouquet to all food, even sweets. Vegetables are usually cooked in it in preference to water. Lots of herbs and lemon juice offset any oiliness, and olive oil is both a health and flavor bonus since it is less fattening and more nourishing than most other cooking fats.

Walnuts, almonds, fresh figs and feta cheese — the list of ingredients that make Greek food special could go on and on. They all add up, though, to a cuisine as vibrant and colorful as the country itself.

SERVES 6-8

SALTED ALMONDS AND CRACKED OLIVES

Olives take on a special flavor when prepared in this way.
Served with crisp toasted almonds, they make a perfect snack.

1lb almonds, unskinned
1 tbsp citric acid
4 tbsps cold water
1 tbsp salt
1lb green olives
2oz coarse salt
1 clove garlic, peeled and left whole
2 sprigs of fresh dill
1 bay leaf
1 sprig thyme
1 tbsp chopped oregano
Vine leaves

1. Spread the almonds in a large roasting pan. Mix the citric acid with the water and sprinkle over the almonds. Stir them around to coat evenly and leave for 10 minutes. Remove them, rinse out the pan and dry it.

2. Place the almonds back into the pan, spread them out and sprinkle with the salt. Shake the pan to coat evenly in salt and then spread the almonds out in an even layer.

3. Cook in a preheated 350°F oven for about 30 minutes, stirring frequently until brown and crisp. Allow them to cool completely before sealing tightly in jars for storage.

4. Hit the green olives gently with a meat mallet or rolling pin to crack the flesh. Alternatively, cut a cross in one side of each olive with a small, sharp knife. Rinse the olives and place them in storage jars. Cover with water and divide the ingredients between the jars. Cover the surface of the olives with the vine leaves.

Step 1 Put the almonds into a large roasting pan and spread into an even layer. Pour the citric acid mixture over the top and stir them to coat evenly.

Step 4 Crack the skin on the olives by gently hitting with a meat mallet or rolling pin.

Step 4 Alternatively, make a small cross on the side of each olive with a sharp knife.

5. Seal the jars to keep in a cool, dark place for 3-4 weeks. To serve, remove the olives and sprinkle with chopped oregano, if desired. Serve with the salted almonds.

Cook's Notes

Preparation
When cracking the olives, take care not to crack the stones. Taste the olives after about 2 weeks; if they have absorbed enough flavor from the various ingredients, they are ready to use.

Cook's Tip
In Greece raw olives are used. If using olives that have already been preserved in brine, they will not need to be stored as long. Use half the quantity of coarse salt.

Time
Preparation takes about 20 minutes, with 3-4 weeks storage time for the olives. Cooking time for the almonds is about 30 minutes.

SERVES 4

FRIED SQUID

Serve this sweet and delicious seafood
as an appetizer or main course. It's
easier to prepare than you think!

1½lb fresh squid
½ cup all-purpose flour
Salt and pepper
Oil for deep-frying
Lemon wedges and parsley for garnishing

1. Hold the body of the squid with one hand and the head with the other and pull gently to separate. Remove the intestines and the quill, which is clear and plastic-like. Rinse the body of the squid inside and outside under cold running water.

2. Cut the tentacles from the head, just above the eye. Separate into individual tentacles.

3. Remove the brownish or purplish outer skin from the body of the squid and cut the flesh into ¼ inch rings.

4. Mix the flour, salt and pepper together on a sheet of paper or in a shallow dish. Toss the rings of squid and the tentacles in the flour mixture to coat. Heat the oil to 350°F and fry the squid, about 6 pieces at a time, saving the tentacles until last. Remove them from the oil when brown and crisp with a draining spoon and place on paper towels.

Step 2 Cut the tentacles from the head just below the eye and separate them into individual pieces.

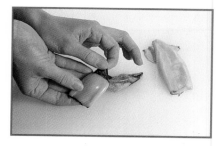

Step 3 Remove the outer skin from the body of the squid and cut the body into thin rings.

Sprinkle lightly with salt and continue with the remaining squid. The pieces will take about 3 minutes to cook. Place on serving dishes and garnish each dish with a wedge of lemon and some parsley.

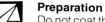

Cook's Notes

Time
Preparation takes about 25 minutes, cooking takes 3 minutes per batch of 6 pieces.

Serving Ideas
Sprinkle the squid with chopped fresh oregano just before serving.

Preparation
Do not coat the pieces of squid too soon before frying or they will become soggy.

Watchpoint
Once the squid is added to the hot oil, cover the fryer as the oil will tend to spatter.

Cook's Tip
If the squid must be re-heated, spread the pieces on wire cooling racks covered with paper towels and place in a slow oven for about 10 minutes. Do not re-fry, as this toughens the squid.

SERVES 4

FRIED EGGPLANT WITH TZATZIKI

The fresh taste of cucumber, mint and yogurt is the
perfect complement to rich, fried eggplant slices.

4 small or 2 medium sized eggplants
½ cup all-purpose flour
Salt and pepper
Vegetable oil for frying

Tzatziki

¼ cucumber, finely chopped or grated
Salt and pepper
1 tbsp olive oil
1 tsp white wine vinegar
1 clove garlic, crushed
½ cup natural yogurt
2 tsps chopped fresh mint
Whole mint leaves for garnishing

1. Wash the eggplants and dry them. Cut into ¼ inch rounds and lightly score the sides with a sharp knife. Sprinkle both sides with salt and leave to drain in a colander or on paper towels for 30 minutes before using.

2. Sprinkle the cucumber lightly with salt and leave in a colander, slightly weighted down, to drain.

3. Rinse both the eggplant slices and cucumber to remove the salt, pat the eggplant slices dry on paper towels and squeeze excess moisture from the cucumber.

4. Mix the salt and pepper together with the flour and coat the eggplant slices well. Heat the oil to 350°F and fry the eggplant slices a few at a time. Remove them with a draining spoon to paper towels and sprinkle lightly with salt. Continue with the remaining slices.

5. Meanwhile, mix the oil and vinegar until well blended and add the crushed garlic. Mix in the yogurt and add the

Step 1 Score the eggplant slices on both sides, sprinkle lightly with salt and leave to drain in a colander or on paper towels.

Step 3 Rinse the cucumber and squeeze, or press between two plates to remove excess moisture.

Step 4 Coat the eggplant slices in seasoned flour and fry them, a few at a time, in hot oil until they turn golden brown. Remove with a draining spoon.

drained cucumber. To serve, arrange the eggplant slices on individual plates or one large plate and add the Tzatziki. Garnish with mint leaves.

Cook's Notes

Cook's Tip
Sprinkling eggplant and cucumber with salt before using draws out excess moisture and bitter juices. Sprinkling deep-fried food lightly with salt while it stands helps to draw out excess fat.

Variation
Zucchini may be used instead of eggplant. Top and tail the zucchini and slice them into 3-4 lengthwise slices. Zucchini do not have to be sprinkled with salt and left to stand.

Time
Preparation takes about 30 minutes, cooking time takes about 2-3 minutes per batch of eggplant slices.

SERVES 6

EGG AND LEMON SOUP

This is one of the best known of all
Greek soups. Diced chicken can be
added to make a more filling soup.

5 cups chicken stock
2 eggs, separated
2 lemons
2oz rice, rinsed

1. Bring the stock to the boil in a large saucepan. When boiling, add the rice and cook for about 10 minutes. Meanwhile, beat the eggs with 1 tbsp cold water for about 3 minutes, or until lightly frothy. Squeeze the lemons for juice and add to the eggs, straining out any seeds. Beat for about 1 minute to blend well.

2. Beat a few spoonfuls of the hot stock into the egg mixture.

Step 1 Squeeze the lemons for juice and add to the egg yolks, straining out any seeds. Beat for about a minute to blend well.

Step 2 Beat a few spoonfuls of the hot stock into the egg mixture.

Step 3 Pour the egg mixture back into the stock in a thin, steady stream, stirring continuously. Do not allow to boil.

3. Gradually add that back to the stock, stirring continuously. Put the soup back over very low heat for about 1-2 minutes, stirring constantly. Do not allow the soup to boil. Serve immediately.

Cook's Notes

Variation
The soup may be served without rice, if desired.

Watchpoint
If the stock boils once the egg is added, it will curdle and the soup will be spoiled.

Time
Preparation takes about 15 minutes, longer if making stock from scratch. Cooking takes about 12-13 minutes. Home made stock will take about 1-1½ hours to make.

Serving Ideas
Sprinkle the soup with chopped fresh oregano or parsley. Also, slice a lemon thinly and float one slice on the top of each serving bowl.

MAKES 1 OMELET

FRESH TOMATO OMELET

For a summer appetizer or lunch, don't forget
about omelets. This one is especially
summery with its ripe tomatoes and fresh herbs.

1lb tomatoes
½ tsp chopped fresh oregano or basil
Salt and pepper
4 eggs, lightly beaten
3 tbsps oil

Step 1 Put the tomatoes immediately into cold water to stop the cooking, and loosen the peels with a small, sharp knife.

1. To make the tomatoes easier to peel, drop them into boiling water and leave them for about 5 seconds. Remove them with a draining spoon and put immediately into ice cold water. Peel with a sharp knife.

2. Cut the tomatoes in half and remove the seeds and juice with a teaspoon. Cut the tomato halves into thin strips.

3. Beat the eggs with the herbs, salt and pepper and heat

Step 2 Remove the seeds and juice from the tomatoes by cutting them in half and scooping the flesh out with a small teaspoon.

Step 1 Dropping tomatoes in boiling water for about 5 seconds will make them easier to peel.

the oil in a large frying pan. When the oil is hot, pour in the eggs and stir with a spatula for about 2-3 minutes, or until the eggs are cooked but not completely set. Sprinkle over the tomato strips and cook until just heated through. Sprinkle with chopped parsley, if desired, before serving.

Cook's Notes

Time
Preparation takes about 25 minutes, cooking about 2-3 minutes.

Preparation
Tomatoes may be prepared well in advance and kept in the refrigerator, tightly covered.

Serving Ideas
This omelet is usually served in the frying pan it was cooked in. Alternatively, cut into wedges to serve.

Variation
One clove of garlic, crushed, may be added to the egg mixture if desired.

SERVES 4

TARAMASALATA

This is a classic Greek appetizer, luxurious
in taste and texture. It is also a
delicious dip for vegetable crudités.

2oz smoked cod's roe
6 slices white bread, crusts removed
1 small onion, finely chopped
1 lemon
6 tbsps olive oil
Black olives and chopped parsley for garnishing

1. Cut the cod's roe in half and scrape the center into a bowl, food processor or blender. Discard the skin. Soak the bread in a bowl of water to soften.

2. Squeeze most of the water from the bread and add it to the roe. Squeeze the lemon and add the juice to the roe and bread, straining to remove the seeds. Add the onion and process until the ingredients form a smooth paste, or beat very well with a wooden spoon.

3. Gradually beat in the oil a drop at a time as if making mayonnaise. If using a blender, it is best to make the Taramasalata in two batches.

4. When all the oil has been added, spoon the Taramasalata into a bowl and chill slightly before serving. Sprinkle with chopped parsley and garnish with black olives.

Step 1 Remove the soft insides of the smoked cod's roe by cutting it in half and scraping with a spoon. Discard the skin.

Step 2 Squeeze the bread to remove excess moisture.

Step 3 Add the oil gradually, drop by drop, beating well continuously, or with the blender or food processor running.

 *Cook's Notes*

 Time
Preparation takes about 15 minutes using a blender or food processor and about 25 minutes if beating by hand.

 Watchpoint
Do not add the oil too quickly or the mixture will curdle. If it does, add a bit more soaked bread and it should come together.

 Variation
If desired, substitute garlic for the onion.

 Preparation
If prepared in advance, remove from the refrigerator about 20 minutes before serving.

 Cook's Tip
Home-made taramasalata is not as pink as that bought commercially.

 Serving Ideas
Warm pitta bread or toast makes a good accompaniment.

SERVES 6-12

SPINACH AND CHEESE PIE

Traditionally made at Easter, this classic
Greek pie is now enjoyed all year round.
Packaged pastry makes it simplicity itself.

1lb package fyllo pastry
1 cup butter, melted
2lbs fresh spinach
3 tbsps olive oil
2 onions, finely chopped
3 tbsps chopped fresh dill
Salt and pepper
3 eggs, slightly beaten
2 cups feta cheese, crumbled

1. Preheat the oven to 375°F. Unfold the pastry on a flat surface and cut it to fit the size of the baking dish to be used. Keep the pastry covered.

2. Tear the stalks off the spinach and wash the leaves well. Shred the leaves with a sharp knife.

3. Heat the oil in a large sauté pan and cook the onions until soft. Add the spinach and stir over a medium heat for about 5 minutes. Turn up the heat to evaporate any moisture.

4. Allow the spinach and onions to cool. Mix in the dill, eggs, salt, pepper, and cheese.

5. Melt the butter and brush the baking dish on the bottom and sides. Brush top sheet of fyllo pastry and place it in the dish. Brush another sheet and place that on top of the first. Repeat to make 8 layers of pastry.

6. Spread on the filling and cover the top with 6 or 7 layers

Step 2 Before washing the spinach, cut off the stalks by holding the leaves firmly and pulling the stems backwards.

Step 5 To assemble the pie, butter the base and sides of the dish and then brush each layer of pastry before stacking them up in the dish.

of pastry, brushing each layer with melted butter. Brush the top layer well and score the pastry in square or diamond shapes. Do not cut through to the bottom layer.

7. Sprinkle with water and bake for 40 minutes or until crisp and golden.

8. Leave the pie to stand for about 10 minutes and then cut through the scoring completely to the bottom layer. Lift out the pieces to a serving dish.

Cook's Notes

Serving Ideas
Serve hot or cold. If serving cold, use olive oil to brush the pastry instead of butter. Serves 6 as a main course, 12 as first course.

Buying Guide
Pastry is available fresh or frozen in large supermarkets or specialty shops.

Time
Preparation takes about 25 minutes, cooking about 40 minutes.

Preparation
The pie can be cooked in advance and reheated for 10 minutes to serve hot.

Cook's Tip
Pastry will go a little soggy when prepared more than a day in advance.

SERVES 6

SAVORY FILLED PIES

Packaged pastry makes these pies very
easy. They make excellent appetizers,
snacks or light meals with a salad.

8oz package fyllo pastry
¾ cup butter, melted
8oz sprue (thin asparagus)
4oz feta cheese
½ cup plain yogurt
2 eggs, beaten
3 green onions, finely chopped
1 tbsp chopped mint
Salt and pepper

1. Use a patty tin with 12 spaces or use 12 ramekin dishes. Cut the pastry in squares large enough to fill the pans or dishes, with enough to overlap the tops by about 1 inch.

2. Layer 3 sheets of pastry, each brushed with melted butter. Cut into 3 inch squares and stack 3 squares, turning each slightly to make a frilled edge. Carefully push the pastry into buttered patty tins or ramekins and keep covered while preparing the filling.

3. Cut the sprue into 1 inch pieces, leaving the tips whole. Cook in boiling salted water until just tender. Rinse under cold water and allow to drain completely. Mix together thoroughly the cheese, yogurt, eggs, onions, mint, salt and pepper. Stir in the drained sprue and fill the pastry to within ½ inch of the top.

4. Bake in a preheated 375°F oven for about 25 minutes or until the pastry is crisp and golden and the filling is set and risen. Allow to cool for about 10 minutes and then remove to a serving dish.

To chop spring onions quickly, cut several into quarters lengthwise and then cut crosswise into small pieces using a very sharp knife.

Step 2 Fill patty tins or ramekin dishes with the prepared pastry to form tartlet cases.

Step 3 The cheese should still be fairly chunky when all the filling ingredients are mixed.

Cook's Notes

Variation
Use spinach instead of asparagus. Cook the spinach briefly and drain it well before combining with the filling ingredients. Substitute other herbs for mint, if desired.

Time
Preparation takes about 30 minutes, cooking takes about 25 minutes.

Cook's Tip
If prepared in advance, reheat for about 5 minutes to serve. The pies can also be served cold.

SERVES 6-8

DOLMADES

In Greece, stuffed vine leaves are not served with a tomato sauce. Try a light egg-lemon sauce or plain yogurt instead.

8oz fresh vine leaves or leaves packed in brine
6oz long-grain rice, cooked
8 green onions, finely chopped
1½ tbsps chopped fresh dill
3 tbsps chopped fresh mint
1 tbsp chopped fresh parsley
½ cup pine nuts
½ cup currants
Salt and pepper
½ cup olive oil
Juice of 1 lemon

1. If using fresh vine leaves, put them into boiling water for about 1 minute. Remove them and drain. If using preserved vine leaves, rinse them and then place in a bowl of hot water for 5 minutes to soak. Strain and pat dry.

2. Mix together all the remaining ingredients except the olive oil and lemon juice. Taste the filling and adjust the seasoning if necessary.

3. Spread the vine leaves out on a flat surface, vein side upwards. Cut off the stems and place about 2 tsps of filling on each leaf, pressing it into a sausage shape.

4. Fold the sides of the leaves over to partially cover the stuffing and roll up as for a jelly roll. Place the rolls seam side down in a large saucepan. Pour over the olive oil and lemon juice.

Step 3 Spread the leaves out on a flat surface. Place spoonfuls of stuffing on the leaves and make into a sausage shape.

Step 4 Fold the sides over the filling and roll up the leaves.

5. Pour hot water over the rolls until it comes about halfway up their sides. Place a plate on top of the rolls to keep them in place, cover the pan and cook slowly for about 40 minutes.

6. Remove the Dolmades to a serving plate and accompany with lemon wedges, black olives and plain yogurt if desired.

Cook's Notes

Time
Preparation takes about 30 minutes, cooking takes about 40 minutes.

Serving ideas
Dolmades may be served either hot or cold, and are ideal for picnics.

Variation
Other ingredients may be used in the filling. Substitute chopped olives, almonds or chopped cooked lamb.

Preparation
Dolmades may be prepared a day before serving. Leave in their liquid in the refrigerator and reheat just before serving.

SERVES 4

GREEK COUNTRY SALAD

Lettuce is cut finely for salads
in Greece. In fact, the finer the shreds of lettuce
the better the salad is considered to be.

2 tbsps olive oil
1 tbsp lemon juice
Salt and ground black pepper
1 clove garlic, crushed
1 Romaine lettuce, well washed
3 tomatoes, sliced
3oz black olives
1 cup feta cheese, diced
½ red pepper, seeded, cored, and sliced
6 peperonata
Fresh or dried oregano

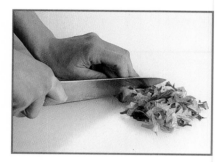

Step 2 To shred the lettuce leaves more quickly, stack them up and use a sharp knife to shred 5 or 6 leaves at a time.

Step 1 If a thick dressing is desired, first whisk the lemon juice, salt, pepper and garlic together in a small bowl and then add the oil gradually, whisking constantly.

Step 3 Use a serrated fruit knife or a bread knife to make the tomatoes easier to slice and the slices neater looking.

1. Whisk the oil, lemon juice, salt, pepper and garlic together until well emulsified. A blender or food processor may be used for this.

2. Stack up 5 or 6 lettuce leaves and shred them finely with a sharp knife.

3. Place the lettuce in the bottom of a serving dish and arrange the other ingredients on top. Spoon over the dressing and sprinkle on the oregano.

Cook's Notes

$ Buying Guide
Peperonata are small whole peppers preserved in brine. They can be bought bottled in delicatessens and some supermarkets.

Variation
Substitute green pepper for red pepper if desired. Other varieties of lettuce may also be used.

 Time
Preparation takes about 10-15 minutes.

SERVES 4

STUFFED TOMATOES

In Greece, stuffed vegetables are
often cooked in olive oil and no
other liquid except the natural juices.

4 large beefsteak tomatoes
6oz cooked rice
2 tsps chopped oregano
1 clove garlic, crushed
2 hard-boiled eggs
4 tbsps feta cheese, grated
1oz black olives, chopped
Salt and pepper
Olive oil

1. Preheat the oven 375°F. Choose tomatoes with nice looking stems and leaves. Cut about 1 inch off the top of each tomato on the stem end. Reserve the tops. Scoop out the pulp and seeds with a small teaspoon into a strainer. Sieve and reserve the juice and pulp.

2. Chop the egg using an egg slicer or a food processor. Mix all the stuffing ingredients together and add some of the reserved tomato pulp and juice.

3. Stuff the tomatoes and place on the caps, leaving some stuffing showing around the edges. Place the tomatoes in a baking dish.

4. Drizzle olive oil over the tops of the tomatoes and bake for about 20 minutes, depending on the ripeness of the tomatoes. Transfer to a serving dish and serve hot or cold.

Step 1 Cut the top off of each tomato on the stem end. Scoop out the pulp and seeds with a small teaspoon or use a serrated grapefruit knife.

Step 2 To chop an egg using an egg slicer, place the egg in the slicer and cut down into rounds.

Step 2 Carefully remove the egg, replace it in the slicer and cut down lengthwise.

Cook's Notes

Variation
Mix the filling ingredients with oil and lemon juice. Stuff the tomatoes and serve them cold.

Time
Preparation takes about 30 minutes, cooking takes about 20 minutes.

Watchpoint
The 20 minute cooking time is just a guide. Watch the tomatoes carefully – they will fall apart easily if overcooked.

Cook's Tip
Keep the hard-boiled eggs in cold water until ready to use. This prevents a gray ring from forming around the yolk.

STUFFED ZUCCHINI

When stuffed vegetables are served with a sauce
in Greece, it is usually a lemon-egg mixture.
Try the sauce with peppers or vine leaves, too.

4 medium-sized zucchini
2 tbsps butter or margarine
1 small onion, finely chopped
4oz ground lamb or beef
1 tsp ground cumin
1 tsp chopped oregano
2 tsps chopped fresh parsley
2 tsps chopped fresh fennel
2oz cooked long-grain rice
2 tbsps grated cheese
Salt and pepper

Egg and Lemon Sauce

2 egg yolks
1 lemon
Salt and pepper

Step 1 Once the zucchini are washed, topped and tailed, cut off a thin strip of skin lengthwise, then hollow out zucchini using a swivel vegetable peeler.

Step 4 Pile the stuffing into the hollowed-out zucchini using a teaspoon.

1. Wash the zucchini well and top and tail them. Using a swivel vegetable peeler, apple corer or a small baller, scoop the middle out of the zucchini, being careful not to damage the outer skins. Leave a thin margin of flesh on the inside for support. Alternatively, slice lengthwise and scoop out the middle.

2. Place the zucchini in boiling salted water and parboil for about 2 minutes. Rinse immediately in cold water and leave to drain. Meanwhile, chop parsley using a large, sharp knife.

3. Prepare the stuffing by softening the onions in half of the butter until they are just transparent. Add the meat and cook until just beginning to brown. Chop up reserved zucchini flesh and add it to the meat. Mix with the remaining stuffing ingredients.

4. Mix the stuffing well and fill the hollow in each zucchini using a small teaspoon.

5. Melt the remaining butter in a large frying pan or sauté pan and, when foaming, place in the zucchini in a single layer. Add water to the pan to come halfway up the sides of the vegetables and cover the pan. Cook over gentle heat for about 20 minutes, basting the zucchini occasionally. Add more water during cooking as necessary.

6. When the zucchini are tender, remove them to a serving dish and keep them warm. Reserve about 4-6 tbsps of the liquid in the pan.

7. To prepare the sauce, beat the egg yolks and the lemon juice together until slightly thickened. Add some of the hot cooking liquid to the eggs and lemon juice and then return the mixture to a small saucepan. Cook over gentle heat, whisking constantly until slightly thickened. Strain over the zucchini before serving. Garnish with sprigs of fresh herbs if desired.

Cook's Notes

Serving Ideas
Stuffed vegetables may be served as a first dish or side dish. The zucchini may be served cold without the sauce.

Watchpoint
Do not allow the sauce to boil once the eggs have been added; it will curdle.

Time
Preparation takes about 30 minutes, cooking takes about 20 minutes.

SERVES 4

STUFFED EGGPLANT

In Greece eggplant are hollowed out from one end and stuffed. Our recipe employs the easy method of cutting them in half.

2 small eggplants
2 tbsps butter or margarine
1 small onion, finely chopped
1 clove garlic, crushed
5oz long-grain rice, cooked
2 tsps oregano
Pinch cinnamon
Salt and pepper
4oz tomatoes, peeled, seeded and
   coarsely chopped

1. Preheat oven to 350°F. Wrap eggplants in paper or foil and bake for 20 minutes to soften. Allow to cool, cut in half and scoop out the pulp leaving a ½ inch border to form a shell.

2. Melt butter or margarine and add the onion and garlic.

Step 1 Cut the cooked eggplants in half and scoop out the pulp with a spoon or melon baller.

Step 1 Leave a layer of pulp on the inside of the skin to form a shell.

Step 2 Chop the pulp roughly before adding to the onions.

Cook to soften slightly. Chop the eggplant pulp roughly and add to the pan. Cook for about 5 minutes and then add the remaining ingredients.

3. Fill the eggplant shells and place them in an ovenproof dish or on a baking sheet. Bake an additional 20 minutes in the oven. Garnish with chopped parsley or other herbs if desired.

Cook's Notes

 Time
Preparation takes about 25 minutes, cooking takes about 40 minutes.

 Preparation
Pre-cooking the eggplant makes it easier to remove the pulp.

 Variation
The eggplants may be sprinkled with dry breadcrumbs and drizzled with olive oil before baking. Add cheese to the filling if desired.

 Serving Ideas
Serve the eggplants hot or cold as a first course or a vegetable side dish.

SERVES 4

STUFFED PEPPERS

Stuffed vegetables are very popular in Mediterranean countries. The addition of lamb to the stuffing makes these a meal in themselves.

4 medium-sized red or green peppers
½ cup olive oil
1 small onion, finely chopped
8oz ground lamb or beef
1 tbsp chopped fresh dill
2 tsps chopped fresh coriander
2 tsps lemon juice
Grated rind of half a lemon
Salt and pepper
½ cup grated cheese
4oz long-grain rice, cooked

1. Wash the peppers and place them in a pan of boiling water. Parboil for about 3 minutes and allow to drain and cool.

2. Cut about 1 inch off the tops and remove the core and seeds. Trim the bottoms of the peppers so that they will stand upright.

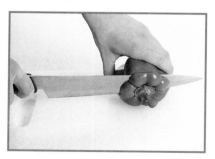

Step 2 Cut the tops off the peppers, but leave the stems attached.

Step 2 Remove the core and seeds with a teaspoon or small knife. If necessary, rinse to remove all the seeds.

Step 2 Slice a thin piece off the bottoms of the peppers so that they will stand level while cooking.

3. Heat 2 tbsps of the oil and cook the onions briefly. Add the lamb and cook until beginning to brown. Add the remaining filling ingredients and stuff the peppers. Put on the tops.

4. Stand the peppers upright close together in a baking dish. Pour over the remaining oil and add enough water to come halfway up the sides of the peppers. Cook 40-45 minutes or until the peppers are tender, basting often. Remove the peppers to a serving dish with a slotted spoon.

Cook's Notes

Preparation
Parboiling the peppers helps to speed up their cooking and makes it easier to remove the core and seeds.

Serving Ideas
Serve the peppers either hot or cold, as a first course or a vegetable side dish.

SERVES 4

OKRA CASSEROLE

This vegetable has always been popular in
Mediterranean cookery and is becoming easier
to find in supermarkets and greengrocers.

4 tbsps olive oil
1 small onion, sliced
8oz okra
6 ripe tomatoes, peeled and quartered
Juice of half a lemon
Salt and pepper
Chopped parsley

1. Heat the olive oil in a sauté pan and cook the onion until soft but not colored.

2. Remove just the stems from the okra, but leave on the tops and tails.

To slice onions, peel and cut in half lengthwise. Place cut side down on chopping board and use a sharp knife to cut across in thin slices.

Cook the onion in the olive oil until soft and transparent.

Step 2 Trim the stems from the tops of the okra, but do not top and tail.

3. Add the okra to the pan and cook for 10 minutes. Add remaining ingredients and cook to heat the tomatoes through. Spoon into a serving dish and serve hot or cold with lamb or chicken.

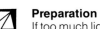

Cook's Notes

Variation
Substitute canned okra, but drain and rinse before use. Cut the cooking time in half. Green beans may be used instead of okra.

Preparation
If too much liquid is left at the end of cooking, remove the vegetables and boil to reduce the sauce.

Cook's Tip
Okra only needs brief cooking or it will become soggy.

SERVES 4

ZUCCHINI AND RED PEPPER SALAD

Salad dressing in Greece is most commonly made from olive oil and·lemon juice instead of vinegar.

1½ lbs very small zucchini
1 red pepper, cored, seeded and thinly sliced
6 tbsps olive oil
Juice and zest of 1 small lemon
Fresh basil
Salt and pepper
Pinch sugar
Whole basil leaves for garnish

1. Top and tail the zucchini. Use a cannelle knife to remove strips of peel from the zucchini. Cut the zucchini in half. If using baby zucchini, top and tail, but leave whole.

2. Place the zucchini and red pepper in boiling salted water and cook for 2 minutes. Allow to drain.

3. Strip the zest from the lemons with a zester. Alternatively, use a swivel peeler to take off strips and then cut the peel in very fine shreds. Blanch for 2 minutes.

4. Mix the oil, lemon juice, chopped basil, salt and pepper and sugar, if desired. Pour over the vegetables while they are still warm and sprinkle with the lemon zest. Garnish with whole basil leaves.

Step 3 Use a lemon zester to make thin strips of lemon peel.

Step 3 As an alternative method, use a swivel peeler to remove thin strips of peel and then cut into thin shreds.

Step 4 Mix the oil, lemon juice, basil, sugar, salt and pepper together well and pour over the warm vegetables.

Cook's Notes

Cook's Tip
If serving the salad cold, rinse the vegetables under cold running water and leave to drain thoroughly

Time
Preparation takes about 25 minutes, cooking takes about 2 minutes.

Serving Ideas
Serve as a side salad, first course, or part of an hors d'oeuvre selection.

SERVES 4

CAULIFLOWER AND OLIVES

Kalamata, where this dish is said to
have originated, is an area of Greece
well known for its black olives.

1 large cauliflower
4 tbsps olive oil
1 onion, cut in rings
½ cup water
Juice of half a lemon
3 tbsps tomato paste
Salt and pepper
3oz black olives
2 tbsps chopped parsley

1. Trim the leaves from the cauliflower and remove the core. Cut into medium sized pieces.

2. Heat the oil and sauté the cauliflower for 1-2 minutes. Remove to a plate and add the onion to the pan. Cook to soften and add the water and lemon juice. Bring to the boil and return the cauliflower to the pan. Cook until tender.

Step 1 Trim the leaves from the cauliflower and remove the core with a small, sharp knife. Cut the flowerets into even-sized pieces

Step 2 When cutting an onion into rings, pierce with a fork and hold the handle to keep the onion steady while slicing.

Step 4 To pit olives, use a cherry pitter or roll them firmly on a flat surface to loosen the stones, then use a swivel peeler to remove them.

3. Remove the cauliflower to a serving dish and add the tomato paste to the liquid and boil to reduce.

4. Pit the olives, chop them roughly and add to the pan. Pour the sauce over the cauliflower and sprinkle with chopped parsley to serve.

Cook's Notes

 Cook's Tip
A bay leaf may be added to the water while cooking the cauliflower. This reduces the cauliflower smell.

Variation
Add strips of tomato pulp with the olives if desired. Green olives may be substituted for black.

 Time
Preparation takes about 25 minutes, cooking takes about 20 minutes.

SERVES 4-6

PEAS AND ARTICHOKES

Fresh peas are a springtime delicacy in
Greece. They are well worth the effort
of shelling for their taste and texture.

2lbs fresh peas
Juice of 1 lemon
Pinch sugar
2 tbsps chopped fresh dill
2 tbsps olive oil
1 small bunch green onions
1 can artichoke hearts, drained
Salt and pepper

1. Shell the peas and put them into boiling salted water with the lemon juice, a pinch of sugar and the dill. Cover and cook for about 20 minutes, or until the peas are tender. Drain and keep warm.

2. Trim the root ends from the green onions and trim down

Step 1 To shell peas, break off stem ends and pull down strings.

Step 1 Press open the pods and push out the peas with finger or thumb.

Step 2 Trim the root ends from the green onions and about 1 inch of the green tops. If the onions are very large, cut in half lengthwise.

the green tops leaving about 1 inch green attached. Heat the olive oil in a saucepan or sauté pan and cook the onions to soften. Cut the artichoke hearts into halves or quarters and add to the onions.

3. Add the peas, salt and pepper and cook for 5 minutes. Serve immediately.

Cook's Notes

Variation
Add peeled and seeded tomatoes, roughly chopped, during the last 5 minutes of cooking. Frozen peas may be substituted for fresh ones, and the cooking time reduced by half.

Cook's Tip
A pinch of sugar added to peas while cooking brings out their flavor.

Serving Ideas
Serve as a vegetable side dish with chicken or lamb.

SERVES 4-6

LEMON CHICKEN

Chicken, lemon and basil is an ideal flavor combination
and one that is used often in Greek cookery.

3lb chicken, jointed
2 tbsps olive oil
2 tbsps butter or margarine
1 small onion, cut in thin strips
2 sticks celery, shredded
2 carrots, cut in julienne strips
1 tbsp chopped fresh basil
1 bay leaf
Juice and grated rind of 2 small lemons
½ cup water
Salt and pepper
Pinch sugar (optional)
Lemon slices for garnishing

1. Heat the oil in a large sauté pan. Add the butter or margarine and, when foaming, place in the chicken, skin side down, in one layer. Brown and turn over. Brown the other side. Cook the chicken in two batches if necessary. Remove the chicken to a plate and set aside.

2. Add the vegetables and cook 2-3 minutes over a moderate heat. Add the basil, bay leaf, lemon juice and rind, water, salt and pepper and replace the chicken. Bring the mixture to the boil.

3. Cover the pan and reduce the heat. Allow to simmer about 35-45 minutes or until the chicken is tender and the juices run clear when the thighs are pierced with a fork.

4. Remove the chicken and vegetables to a serving dish and discard the bay leaf. The sauce should be thick, so boil

To cut the onion in thin strips, first cut in half through the root end. Using a sharp knife, follow the natural lines in the onion and cut through neatly to the flat base. Cut off the root end and the onion will fall apart in strips.

To make the carrots easier to cut into julienne strips, first cut them into rect-angular blocks.

Cut the carrot blocks into thin slices and then stack them up to cut into strips quickly.

to reduce if necessary. If the sauce is too tart, add a pinch of sugar. Spoon the sauce over the chicken to serve and garnish with the lemon slices.

Cook's Notes

 Watchpoint
Pat the chicken with paper towels to make sure it is really dry or it will spit when browning.

 Variation
Use limes instead of lemons and oregano instead of basil.

 Serving Ideas
There is a flat, square shaped pasta in Greece that is often served with chicken dishes. Rice is also a good accompaniment, along with a green salad.

 Time
Preparation takes about 30 minutes, cooking takes about 45-55 minutes total, including browning of chicken.

SERVES 4-6

CHICKEN WITH OLIVES

This is a chicken sauté dish for olive lovers. Use more or less of them as your own taste dictates.

3lb chicken, jointed
2 tbsps olive oil
2 tbsps butter or margarine
1 clove garlic, crushed
½ cup white wine
½ cup chicken stock
Salt and pepper
2 tbsps chopped parsley
20 pitted black and green olives
4 zucchini, cut in ½ inch pieces

1. Heat the oil in a large sauté pan and add the butter or margarine. When foaming, add the chicken skin side down in one layer. Brown one side of the chicken and turn over to brown the other side. Cook the chicken in two batches if necessary.

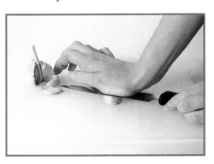

To peel a garlic clove easily, first crush it gently with the side of a large knife. The peel will split, making it easier to remove.

To cut the zucchini quickly into chunks, first top and tail them, then cut them in half if small, or quarters if large, lengthwise. Gather the strips together and cut crosswise into chunks of the desired size.

Step 1 Cook the chicken, skin side down first, until golden brown.

2. Turn the chicken skin side up and add the garlic, wine, stock, salt and pepper. Bring to the boil, cover the pan and allow to simmer over gentle heat for about 30-35 minutes.

3. Add the zucchini and cook 10 minutes. Once the chicken and zucchini are done, add the olives and cook to heat through. Add the parsley and remove to a dish to serve.

Cook's Notes

 Time
Preparation takes about 25 minutes, cooking takes about 50-55 minutes.

 Serving Ideas
Serve with rice or pasta and tomato salad.

 Variation
Artichoke hearts may be used in place of the zucchini.

SERVES 4

MARINATED CHICKEN WITH WALNUT SAUCE

Offer your guests a walnut sauce that tastes
delicious and is very easy to make.

2 2lb chickens, cut in half
½ cup olive oil
Juice and grated rind of 2 lemons
1 tbsp chopped fresh oregano
Pinch ground cumin
1 tbsp chopped fresh parsley
2 tsps chopped fresh thyme
Salt and pepper
Pinch sugar

Walnut Sauce

2 cloves garlic, peeled and roughly chopped
4 slices bread, crusts removed and soaked in water for 10
    minutes
2 tbsps white wine vinegar
Salt and pepper
4-5 tbsps olive oil
1-2 tbsps water (optional)
¾ cup ground walnuts

Step 1 Remove the backbone from the chickens using a pair of sharp poultry shears or a cleaver.

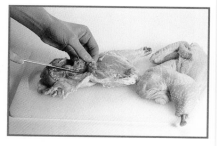

Step 1 Cut away some of the ribcage to make the chickens easier to flatten with a meat mallet or rolling pin.

1. Remove the backbones from the chickens with poultry shears. Bend the legs backwards to break the ball and socket joint. Cut away some of the ribcage with a sharp knife. Flatten the chickens slightly with a meat mallet or rolling pin. Mix together the marinating ingredients in a large, shallow dish or a large plastic bag. Place in the chicken and turn to coat. If using a plastic bag, fasten securely and place in a dish to catch any drips. Refrigerate for at least 4 hours or overnight.

2. Place the chicken on a broiler pan and cook under low heat for about 30 minutes, basting frequently. Raise the heat and cook for a further 10 minutes, skin side up, to brown nicely.

3. Meanwhile, place the garlic in a food processor and squeeze the bread to remove the water. Add the bread to the food processor along with the vinegar. With the machine running, pour the oil through the funnel in a thin, steady stream. Add water if necessary to bring the sauce to coating consistency. Add salt and pepper and stir in the walnuts by hand. When the chicken is cooked, remove it to a serving dish and pour over any remaining marinade. Serve with the walnut sauce.

Cook's Notes

Cook's Tip
If broiler does not have an adjustable setting, pre-cook the chicken in the oven for about 30 minutes and then broil for the remaining time until done.

Serving Ideas
Garnish with lemon wedges and sprigs of parsley or other fresh herbs, if desired. Serve with rice and a green or tomato salad.

Time
Preparation takes about 30 minutes plus marinating time, cooking takes about 40 minutes.

SERVES 4-6

MOUSSAKA

There are many different recipes for this casserole dish. This one is light, with no potatoes and a soufflé-like topping.

2 large eggplant, thinly sliced
Oil for frying
2 tbsps butter or margarine
2 onions, thinly sliced
1 clove garlic, crushed
1lb ground lamb
14oz canned tomatoes
2 tbsps tomato paste
Salt and pepper
2 tsps chopped oregano
¼ tsp ground cinnamon
¼ tsp ground cumin

White Sauce

4 tbsps butter or margarine
4 tbsps flour
2 cups milk
Salt and white pepper
2 tbsps grated cheese
2 eggs, separated

Topping

4 tbsps finely grated cheese
4 tbsps dry breadcrumbs

1. Preheat the oven to 350°F. Heat the oil in a large frying pan and fry the eggplant slices for about 3 minutes. Remove them and drain on paper towels.

2. Pour the oil from the pan and melt the butter or margarine. Fry the onion and garlic for about 4 minutes, or until golden brown. Add the lamb and cook for about 10 minutes, breaking up well with a fork. Add the tomatoes and

Step 5 To assemble the Moussaka, layer up the meat and eggplants, ending with an even layer of eggplants on top.

their juice, tomato paste, oregano, spices, salt and pepper. Bring to the boil, cover the pan and allow to simmer over gentle heat for 20 minutes.

3. To prepare the white sauce, melt the butter in a deep saucepan and stir in the flour off the heat. Gradually pour in the milk and add a pinch of salt and pepper. Whisk or beat well and return the pan to the heat. Cook over moderate heat, stirring continuously until thickened. Add the cheese and allow the sauce to cool slightly. Beat the egg yolks with one spoonful of the hot sauce and then gradually add to the sauce.

4. Whip the egg whites until stiff peaks form and fold a spoonful into the hot sauce mixture. Make sure it is thoroughly incorporated and then gently fold in the remaining egg whites.

5. Layer the meat mixture and the eggplant slices in an ovenproof casserole, ending with a layer of eggplant. Spoon the white sauce on top and sprinkle on the topping of cheese and breadcrumbs. Cook for about 45 minutes to 1 hour or until the topping has risen slightly and formed a golden crust on top. Allow to stand for about 5 minutes before serving to make cutting easier.

Cook's Notes

Cook's Tip
If preparing and assembling the moussaka in advance, add whole eggs to the white sauce and omit the separate whisking of egg whites.

Economy
Use left-over roast lamb, minced in a food processor or cut into small dice by hand.

Time
Preparation takes about 30 minutes, cooking takes about 45 minutes to 1 hour.

SERVES 4

LAMB KEBABS

Meat kebabs are the typical Greek dish and these have all the
characteristic flavors — oregano, garlic, lemon and olive oil.

1½lbs lean lamb from the leg or neck fillet
Juice of 1 large lemon
6 tbsps olive oil
1 clove garlic, crushed
1 tbsp chopped fresh oregano
1 tbsp chopped fresh thyme
Salt and pepper
2 medium-sized onions
Fresh bay leaves

1. Trim the meat of excess fat and cut it into 2 inch cubes.
Mix together the remaining ingredients except the bay
leaves and the onions. Pour the mixture into a shallow dish
or into a large plastic bag.

2. Place the meat in the dish or the bag with the marinade
and turn to coat completely. If using a bag, tie securely and
place in a dish to catch any drips. Leave to marinate for at
least four hours, or overnight.

Step 1 Cut the
meat into even-
sized cubes.

Step 2 Marinade
may be poured
into a plastic bag.
Add the meat, tie
the bag securely
and shake gently
to coat the meat
completely. Place
the bag in a dish
to catch any
drips.

Step 3 Thread
the meat and bay
leaves onto
skewers and slip
the onion rings
over the meat.

3. To assemble the kebabs, remove the meat from the
marinade and thread onto skewers, alternating with the
fresh bay leaves.

4. Slice the onions into rings and slip the rings over the
meat on the skewers.

5. Place the kebabs on the broiler pan and broil for about
3 minutes per side under a preheated broiler. Baste the
kebabs often. Alternatively, grill over hot coals. Pour over
any remaining marinade to serve.

 Cook's Notes

Time
Preparation takes about 20
minutes plus marinating time.
Cooking takes about 3 minutes per
side, but will vary according to desired
doneness.

Variation
Rump or sirloin steak may be
used in place of the lamb. The
cooking time will have to be increased,
but cook until desired doneness is
reached.

 Serving Ideas
A Greek country salad and
rice make good accompan-
iments. Kebabs may also be served
with stuffed vegetables.

SERVES 6-8

LAMB WITH PASTA AND TOMATOES

Lamb appears in many different guises in Greek cuisine;
this recipe offers a delicious blend of subtle tastes.

1 leg or shoulder of lamb
2 cloves garlic, peeled and cut into thin slivers
4 tbsps olive oil
1lb fresh tomatoes or 14oz canned tomatoes
1 tbsp chopped fresh oregano
Salt and pepper
2 cups lamb or beef stock or water
8oz pasta shells, spirals or other shapes
Finely grated Parmesan cheese

1. Cut slits at about 2 inch intervals all over the lamb. Insert small slivers of garlic into each slit. Place the lamb in a large baking dish and rub the surface with the olive oil.

2. Cook in a preheated oven at 425°F for about 50 minutes, basting occasionally.

3. Meanwhile, parboil the pasta for about 5 minutes and rinse in hot water to remove the starch.

Step 1 Cut slits at intervals all over the lamb with a small, sharp knife. Insert slivers of garlic into each cut.

Step 4 Mix the tomatoes with oregano, salt and pepper and pour over the lamb.

Step 4 Once the pasta is added to the lamb, take the dish out of the oven occasionally and stir so that the pasta cooks evenly.

4. Turn the meat over and add the stock or water, pasta and additional seasoning. Mix the tomatoes with the oregano, salt and pepper and pour over the lamb. Stir well. Cook an additional 20-30 minutes, stirring the pasta occasionally to ensure even cooking.

5. When the pasta is completely cooked, turn the lamb over again and sprinkle with cheese to serve. Serve directly from the dish or transfer to a large, deep serving plate.

Cook's Notes

Cook's Tip
If the meat reaches desired doneness before the pasta is cooked, remove it to a serving plate and keep it warm. Continue cooking the pasta, covering the dish to speed things up.

Variation
The dish can be made without tomatoes, if desired. Beef can be substituted for the lamb and the cooking time increased.

Time
Preparation takes about 20 minutes, cooking takes about 1 hour 35 minutes.

SERVES 4

FRIED FISH WITH GARLIC SAUCE

Fish in such an attractive shape makes an
excellent first course.

2lbs fresh anchovies or whitebait
1 cup of all-purpose flour
4-6 tbsps cold water
Pinch salt
Oil for frying

Garlic Sauce

4 slices bread, crusts trimmed, soaked in water for 10
    minutes
4 cloves garlic, peeled and roughly chopped
2 tbsps lemon juice
4-5 tbsps olive oil
1-2 tbsps water (optional)
Salt and pepper
2 tsps chopped fresh parsley
Lemon wedges for garnishing (optional)

1. Sift the flour into a deep bowl with a pinch of salt.
Gradually stir in the water in the amount needed to make a
very thick batter.

2. Heat enough oil for frying in a large, deep pan. A deep-
sided sauté pan is ideal.

3. Take 3 fish at a time and dip them into the batter together.
Press their tails together firmly to make a fan shape.

4. Lower them carefully into the oil. Fry in several batches
until crisp and golden. Continue in the same way with all the
remaining fish.

Step 3 Dip three
fish at a time into
the batter and
when coated
press the tails
together firmly to
form a fan shape.

Step 4 Lower the
fish carefully into
the hot oil to
preserve the
shape.

5. Meanwhile, squeeze out the bread and place in a food
processor with the garlic and lemon juice. With the processor running, add the oil in a thin, steady stream. Add
water if the mixture is too thick and dry. Add salt and pepper
and stir in the parsley by hand. When all the fish are cooked,
sprinkle lightly with salt and arrange on serving plates with
some of the garlic sauce and lemon wedges, if desired.

Cook's Notes

Time
Preparation takes about 30
minutes, cooking takes about
3 minutes per batch for the fish.

Preparation
Coat the fish in the batter just
before ready for frying.

Cook's Tip
The fish should be eaten
immediately after frying. If it is
necessary to keep the fish warm, place
them on a wire cooling rack covered
with paper towels in a slow oven with
the door open. Sprinkling fried food
lightly with salt helps to absorb excess
fat.

Variation
Fish may be dipped in the
batter and fried singly if
desired. Other fish, such as smelt or
sardines, may also be used. Use thin
strips of cod or halibut as well. Vary the
amount of garlic in the sauce to your
own taste.

SERVES 4
BAKED RED MULLET WITH GARLIC AND TOMATOES

This is a fish that appears often in Mediterranean cookery.

4 even-sized red mullet
3 tbsps olive oil
3 tbsps dry white wine
1 lemon
2 cloves garlic, crushed
Salt and pepper
12oz fresh tomatoes, thinly sliced or 14oz canned
    tomatoes, strained
Sprigs of fresh dill for garnish

1. Preheat the oven to 375°F. First scale the fish by running the blunt edge of a large knife over the skin of the fish going from the tail to the head.

2. Using a filleting knife, cut along the belly of the fish from just under the head to the vent, the small opening near the tail. Clean out the cavity of the fish, leaving in the liver if desired. Rinse the fish well inside and out and pat dry.

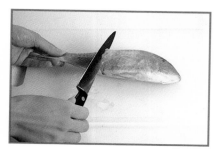

Step 1 To scale the fish, hold it by the tail and run the blunt side of a knife down the length of the body from the tail to the head.

Step 2 To gut the fish, cut with a filleting knife from just under the head to the vent and remove the insides of the fish.

Step 3 Rinse the fish well under cold running water and, using kitchen scissors, trim the tail and fins.

3. Trim the fins and neaten the tail with kitchen scissors. Place the fish head to tail in an ovenproof dish. Mix the oil and the wine together and squeeze the juice from one of the lemons. Add the garlic, salt and pepper and pour over the fish. Place on the tomato slices or if using canned tomatoes, crush them slightly and spoon over. Bake for about 25 minutes, basting frequently until the fish is tender. Garnish with dill.

Cook's Notes

Variation
Add thinly sliced fennel to the fish before baking, in addition to the tomatoes. Substitute other fish such as sea bass, gray mullet, or fish steaks such as cod or halibut.

Time
Preparation takes about 20 minutes, cooking takes about 25 minutes.

Cook's Tip
Red mullet spoils quickly, so use on the day of purchase.

SERVES 4

GRILLED FISH

Grilling fish with herbs and lemon is one of the most delightful ways of preparing it, and is particularly common in the Greek Islands.

2 large bream or other whole fish
Fresh thyme and oregano
Olive oil
Lemon juice
Salt and pepper
Lemon wedges
Vine leaves

1. Preheat a broiler. Gut the fish and rinse it well. Pat dry and sprinkle the cavity with salt, pepper and lemon juice. Place sprigs of herbs inside.

2. Make 3 diagonal cuts on the sides of the fish with a sharp knife. Place the fish on the broiler rack and sprinkle with olive oil and lemon juice.

3. Cook on both sides until golden brown and crisp. This should take about 8-10 minutes per side, depending on the thickness of the fish.

To make perfect lemon wedges, first cut the ends off the lemons, then cut in 4 or 8 wedges and remove the membrane and seeds.

Step 1 Open the cavity of the fish and sprinkle with salt, pepper and lemon juice.

Step 2 Use a sharp knife to make diagonal cuts on both sides of each fish.

4. If using vine leaves preserved in brine, rinse them well. If using fresh vine leaves, pour over boiling water and leave to stand for about 10 minutes to soften slightly. Drain and allow to cool. Line a large serving platter with the vine leaves and when the fish is cooked place it on top of the leaves. Serve surrounded with lemon wedges.

Cook's Notes

Time
Preparation takes about 20 minutes, cooking takes about 16-20 minutes, depending upon the size of the fish.

Cook's Tip
When broiling large whole fish, slit the skin on both sides to help the fish cook evenly.

Variation
The fish may be wrapped in vine leaves before broiling. This keeps the fish moist and adds extra flavor. Other fish suitable for cooking by this method are red mullet, trout, sea bass, gray mullet, sardines, herring or mackerel.

Preparation
If desired, the fish may be cooked on an outdoor barbecue grill. Wait until the coals have white ash on the top and be sure to oil the racks before placing on the fish, or use a special wire cage for cooking fish.

SERVES 4

FIGS AND CURRANTS WITH ORANGE

Fruit is the most popular sweet in Greece, and fresh figs are a favorite choice.

4 fresh figs
Small bunches of fresh redcurrants
6 oranges
1 tsp orange flower water

1. Cut the stalks off the tops of the figs but do not peel them.

2. Cut the figs in quarters but do not cut completely through the base. Open the figs out like flowers and stand them on their bases on serving dishes. Arrange small bunches of redcurrants on the figs. Squeeze the juice from 2 of the oranges. Peel and segment the other 4 and arrange segments around each fig.

Step 2 Peel the oranges and cut into segments.

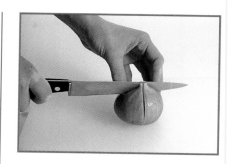

Step 2 With a small, sharp knife, cut the figs into quarters, but not all the way through the base.

Step 2 Open the figs out like flowers.

3. Pour over the orange juice mixed with the orange flower water and chill before serving.

Variation
Orange flower water may be omitted if desired. Blackcurrants may be substituted for the redcurrants.

Serving Ideas
Yogurt and honey may be served as an accompaniment.

Time
Preparation takes about 15 minutes.

SERVES 6-8

BAKLAVA

Fyllo pastry is used for sweet dishes as well as savory ones. Serve baklava in small portions; it is buttery and rich.

Syrup

1½ cups granulated sugar
6 tbsps liquid honey
1½ cups water
1 tbsp lemon juice
1 tbsp orange flower water

Pastry

1lb package fyllo pastry
1 cup unsalted butter, melted
1 cup chopped walnuts, almonds or pistachio nuts
½ tsp ground cinnamon
1½ tbsps sugar

1. First make the syrup by combining all the ingredients in a heavy-based saucepan. Place over low heat until the sugar dissolves. Stir occasionally. Once the sugar is dissolved, raise the heat and allow the syrup to boil until it is thick enough to coat a spoon. This should take about 2 minutes. Allow the syrup to cool and then chill thoroughly.

2. Preheat the oven to 350°F. Brush a rectangular baking dish, about 12x18 inches, with some of the melted butter. Place about 8 of the pastry sheets in the dish, brushing the top of each with melted butter.

3. Mix the nuts, sugar and cinnamon together and spread half of the mixture over the top of the pastry. Place two more layers of the buttered pastry on top and then cover with the remaining nuts. Layer up the remaining pastry, brushing each layer with butter.

Step 1 Cook the syrup slowly until the sugar dissolves and the liquid looks clear.

Step 1 Bring the syrup to a rapid boil and allow to boil for about 2 minutes, until thick enough to coat a spoon.

4. With a sharp knife, score a diamond pattern in the top. Sprinkle the pastry with water to keep it moist and prevent curling. Bake for 30 minutes and then raise the oven temperature to 425°F. Continue baking for 10-15 minutes longer, or until the pastry is cooked and the top is golden brown and crisp.

5. Remove the pastry from the oven and immediately pour over the syrup. Leave the pastry to cool and when thoroughly cold, cut into diamond shapes to serve.

Cook's Notes

Time
Preparation takes about 30 minutes, cooking takes about 40-45 minutes. Preparation time does not include chilling the syrup or the pastry.

Cook's Tip
Baklava may be made several days in advance and kept in the refrigerator. Leave at room temperature for about 20 minutes before serving.

Watchpoint
When boiling the syrup, watch it constantly. Sugar syrups can turn to caramel very quickly. If this happens, discard the syrup and begin again.

HONEY SHORTBREAD

Sweets in a honey syrup are quite common
in Greece. Use hymettus honey, which is
dark and fragrant, for authenticity.

3 cups all-purpose flour, sifted
1 tsp baking powder
1 tsp bicarbonate of soda
1 cup olive oil
¼ cup sugar
½ cup brandy
4 tbsps orange juice
1 tbsp grated orange rind
½ cup chopped walnuts
1 tsp cinnamon

Syrup

1 cup honey
½ cup sugar
1 cup water

1. Preheat the oven to 350°F. Sift flour, baking powder and soda together.

2. Combine oil, sugar, brandy, orange juice and rind in a large bowl or food processor. Gradually add the dry ingredients, running the machine in short bursts. Work just until the mixture comes together.

Step 2 Add the dry ingredients to the liquid ingredients gradually, combining well after each addition.

Step 3 Flour hands well and shape mixture into ovals. Place well apart on baking sheets.

Step 5 Dip the shortbread into the syrup and sprinkle on nuts and cinnamon while still wet.

3. Grease and flour several baking sheets. Shape the shortbread mixture into ovals about 3 inches long. Place well apart on prepared baking sheets and cook about 20 minutes. Cool on the baking sheet.

4. Mix the syrup ingredients together and bring to the boil. Boil rapidly for 5 minutes to thicken. Allow to cool.

5. Dip the cooled shortbread into the syrup and sprinkle with nuts and cinnamon. Allow to set slightly before serving.

Cook's Notes

❄ Freezing
Do not dip the biscuits in syrup. Wrap them well, label and store for up to 2 months. Defrost thoroughly before coating with syrup, nuts and cinnamon.

❗ Watchpoint
If the mixture is overworked it becomes too soft to shape and will spread when baked. Chill in the refrigerator to firm up.

🕐 Time
Preparation takes about 20 minutes, cooking takes 10 minutes for the syrup to boil and about 20 minutes for the biscuits to bake.

INDEX

ACKNOWLEDGMENT
The publishers wish to thank the following suppliers
for their kind assistance:
Corning Ltd for providing Pyrex and other cookware.
Habasco International Ltd for the loan of basketware.
Stent (Pottery) Ltd for the loan of glazed pottery oven-
to-table ware.

Compiled by Judith Ferguson
Photographed by Peter Barry
Designed by Philip Clucas and Sara Cooper
Recipes Prepared for Photography by
Jacqueline Bellefontaine